RIVERS

Troll Associates

RIVERS

by Laurence Santrey

Illustrated by Lynn Sweat

Troll Associates

Library of Congress Cataloging in Publication Data

Santrey, Laurence.
  Rivers.

  Summary: A discussion of rivers, their types, how they
begin, their effect on the land they flow through, and
their uses.
  1. Rivers—Juvenile literature. [1. Rivers] I. Sweat,
Lynn, ill. II. Title.
GB1203.8.S26 1985   551.48 '3   84-8818
  ISBN 0-8167-0210-1 (lib. bdg.)
  ISBN 0-8167-0211-X (pbk.)

A river can be a rushing torrent of icy water that bubbles and bursts in spray and foam. A river can be a thin ribbon of water that cuts a groove through hard rock. A river can be a slow, steady flow so wide that you can't see from one side to the other. A river can be as straight as a ruler, or as twisting as a snake slithering through grass. It can be clear and blue, or muddy and brown. And one river can be all of these things in different places along its path.

All rivers, everywhere in the world, begin the same way—as water that falls from the sky in the form of rain or snow, or as water from melting glaciers.

The water runs over the ground to lower places, and as it runs over the ground in tiny trickles, it keeps moving downhill. Soon a few trickles join together to become a stream. Then several streams come together, growing deeper and wider until they form a river. And the water keeps on flowing until it finally runs out to the sea.

Most of the great rivers of the world begin near the tops of very high mountains. There, the winter brings heavy snowfalls. Then, as spring warmth melts the snow, the water begins to trickle down the mountain, joining the waters of the spring rains.

The trickles become a rivulet, racing over the steep ground in a fast-flowing current. As this stream of water speeds along, it wears away rocks and soil in a process called *erosion*.

The pebbles and sand carried along by the fast-moving stream rub against the sides and bottom of the stream's channel. This rubbing makes the channel deeper and wider. Other streams rushing downhill join in, and all together they become a river. The river moves over the steep ground, picking up more rock and soil sediment.

When it reaches a place where the land isn't so steep, the current slows. Some of the sediment falls to the bottom, or bed, of the river channel. As the sediment piles up, the river must begin to change its course. It curves around the newly built-up ground, always moving toward lower ground.

Scientists divide rivers into three types—
young, mature, and old. These words, however, don't describe the age of rivers. There
are young rivers that have been flowing
over the Earth for more years than some old
rivers. The words young, mature, and old
describe how different rivers look and flow.

A young river flows quickly over a steep and bumpy riverbed. Young rivers have rapids—places where water swirls and tumbles over rocks. And young rivers also may have waterfalls, where the water plunges straight down with great force until it reaches a lower level.

13

The racing waters of a young river cut a
sharp, V-shaped valley in the land. The
V-shaped cut grows deeper as the young
river scrapes away the land like a liquid
knife. As this is happening, other forces of

nature are working on the river valley. Wind and rain erode the soil and rock on the sides above the river. The mile-deep Grand Canyon of the southwestern United States was carved in just this way.

A river that flows over ground that is not steep flows more slowly than a young river. It moves in gentle curves across land that is almost flat, or just a bit hilly. This is a mature river. As a mature river weaves its way across the land, it cuts a U-shaped channel in the ground. The curves of a mature river, called *meanders*, are always changing. These changes take place as the river picks up pieces of soil and sand from its banks and bed and deposits this sediment downriver.

Sometimes there are rocks or tree roots at the edge of the riverbed. The slow-moving water cannot move them, so it goes around these barriers. As it does, it deposits some of the sediment it had carried.

A bump of sedimentary land begins to grow on that bank of the river, and the water is forced to go around it. Then the water begins to wear away the bank on the opposite side of the river.

The built-up side of a mature river is a natural *levee*. A levee is a raised area of land that keeps a river from overflowing its banks. However, the worn-away side may be flooded during heavy rains. To prevent this from happening, people often build artificial levees of sand or stone or wood.

Sometimes rivers are used as boundary lines between states or countries. Problems may arise if such a river changes its course. For example, the Rio Grande River forms part of the boundary between the United States and Mexico. But when the boundary lines were first drawn, parts of the river flowed in different places from where they flow today. Over the course of years, as the river changed its course, land that belonged to Mexico became part of the United States. And land that belonged to the United States became part of Mexico. Finally, the boundary lines had to be redrawn.

As a river continues to widen, its flow slows even more. In time, it may become very slow-moving and wide, like the Mississippi River of North America or the Nile River of Egypt. Rivers like these are called old rivers. They have gently sloping beds, broad valleys, and flood plains that are often very wide.

Flood plains are low stretches of land that may, from time to time, be flooded by the waters of an old river. For this reason, homes are not usually built on a flood plain. But the land itself is excellent for farming, since the sediment deposited by the flooding river is very rich in minerals. One reason why agriculture flourished in ancient Egypt and Mesopotamia was because of the fertile flood plains.

The place where a river empties into a lake or ocean is called the river *mouth*. Old rivers often form *deltas* at their mouths. A delta is a wide, fan-shaped piece of land made up of sediment the river has carried along its course.

The city of New Orleans, Louisiana, is built on the Mississippi River delta. The country of the Netherlands is located on a very large delta that was formed where three rivers empty into the North Sea.

An *estuary* is a broad area where a river and ocean meet. Many estuaries contain tidal marshes, shallow areas where fresh water and salt water mix. Tidal marshes are home for grasses and reeds, young fish, shellfish, and many kinds of birds and animals.

All along their lengths, rivers support many different kinds of plants and animals. These plants and animals—from the smallest to the largest—are all linked together in a complex *food chain*.

A food chain never ends. It starts with tiny, one-celled plants called algae. The algae are food for small fish, snails, insects, and other river creatures. These, in turn, are food for larger fish, birds, and land animals. And the fish, birds, and animals —as well as many plants—become food for people.

We use rivers in many ways. We fish in rivers, drink their waters, use them for transportation, and irrigate our farm lands with them. We have harnessed the power of the river's fast-flowing waters to produce electricity. And we pipe river water many miles to distant cities and farms.

At the same time, in many parts of the world, we have also dumped chemical wastes, sewage, and other harmful substances into rivers. So over the years, many rivers have become badly polluted.

But we are learning how—with care and effort—to make our rivers healthy and beautiful again. Our rivers are life-giving, natural treasures. We must do all we can to keep them that way!